FESTIVALS
IN THE NEW AGE

FESTIVALS
IN THE NEW AGE

David Spangler

Findhorn Foundation

Edited by:
Roy McVicar

Designed by:
Frank Stong and Irena Majcen

Illustrations by:
Irena Majcen: (cover, pages 5, 37, 65, 75)
David Nez: (pages 11, 25, 85)
Aidan Meehan (page 51)
David Clapham (page 6)

Calligraphy by:
Anne Zontine

Published by:
The Findhorn Foundation
The Park, Findhorn Bay
Forres, Moray, Scotland

Printed by:
Findhorn Publications

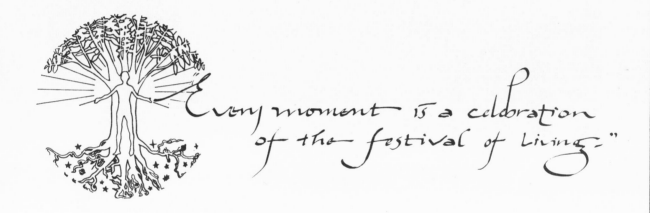

"Every moment is a celebration of the festival of living."

Contents

Most of the following material represents information shared by David Spangler with the Findhorn Community during the years of 1970—1973. As such, it represents a stage in the growth of consciousness of both the community and of David. It was given in response to specific needs or questions existing within Findhorn during those years, and it was intended to be a foundation for further exploration and understanding. In no fashion does it represent a final statement on any of the principles mentioned. It is a particular reflection in time and space of the Universal and has value not only in its particularity but in its use as a guide into that Universal, within which specific words, phrases and teachings must give way to the experience of the truth of Being and Reality. If this material assists you as such a guide, then it fulfils its purpose; it will have taken you beyond itself. If not, then perhaps it may still serve as an indication of where your guide may be by providing you with an experience of where it is not.

Findhorn Publications

Introduction

Festivals have played a large and important part in the life of all people in all ages upon Earth.

Some of these festivals have related to the cycle of natural life, and have enabled man to understand and harness the forces of life.

Others are related to the movement of personal and spiritual life of Man and in a real way symbolise the powers on which he may draw in order to live more fully.

In this book, based on lectures which he gave, David Spangler penetrates to the heart of FESTIVAL in order to make clear what is the meaning and purpose of celebrating the festivals in the New Age, and to help Man to experience in his living the immense spiritual powers which are his true heritage.

A festival
is a time of joy —,
a time of sharing
a time of song
and Mirth
and dance,
all of which is simply
the outer manifestation
of an inner state of being

Chapter 1

Festivals: Their Nature and Their Purpose

In ancient days, the cultures that Man created quite often celebrated great festivals, times when the community would come together in a collective act of worship, of joy and of symbolic ritual in order to invoke various forces of Nature. These festivals were also times for dramatising and identifying the energies and events that characterised certain natural periods. The early festivals, therefore, were Nature orientated. They were geared to the two equinoxes of spring and autumn and to the two solstices of winter and summer, and in each of these festivals recognition was made of the particular quality or characteristic which that period of time represented in the cyclic and rhythmic life of Earth and its natural kingdoms. Through the use of festivals, a greater power of integration was released within the consciousness of the people—integration amongst themselves because of their collective experience, and integration through identification with the forces of Nature.

In many so-called primitive cultures, men would identify themselves with elements from their environment. They would portray various animals or the vital forces such as wind and rain, the sun and the power of life vivifying the seeds within the soil. In so doing, Man sought to harness these energies and channel them through his ritual, bringing them to a focus where they could greatly assist him in his own endeavours, and also affirming his place in the natural scheme of things. In this sense, the ancient festivals were festivals of ecology in which Man realised and demonstrated

12

his role in the dance of life.

As Man's cultures became increasingly sophisticated and as he began to develop human aspects of life, other kinds of festivals developed, festivals to celebrate the lives of great men and women, festivals to celebrate important events in civic and in religious history, festivals to celebrate cultural and artistic impulses.

The use of festivals as an integrating and synthesising force, and as a means of psychologically and spiritually unifying Man and his environment, is not as well understood in modern western culture as it was in the past. In the New Age festivals will again become an important part of human experience, but with this difference, that those who participate in them will do so as an outgrowth of their own recognition and response to the festival within themselves and not simply as participants in a ritual, a drama or a dance which has no meaning beyond the activity itself.

One way of looking at life is to say that everything we do and everything we experience is a symbol behind which lies a greater reality, a reality that cannot be expressed verbally, intellectually or physically, but which is there nonetheless. There are those individuals who, by one means or another, have penetrated through the symbolic forms of their environment, have touched this reality and have experienced its infinite power and its infinite wholeness. Everything we do in life may be looked upon as a result of that which has emanated from this unseen reality. If we understand these results, if we understand ourselves and our environment properly, then we can begin to understand this other universe.

Festivals are a means of doing this, for they cultivate within human consciousness an understanding of the symbolic nature of living: that all of life on form levels is, as it were, the unfolding of a great story. It is a dance, a song, a drama. and it is human destiny to move beyond the stage, beyond the script, to become one with the author, the playwright, the composer, the life of the inner universe. However, in order to do so, one must see the outer world with a certain detachment. One must see it as if it were a device for communicating the unseen. A person who can approach his life and his world as if it were a vast allegory (nonetheless real and important for being that, but not as an ultimate end, only as an expression of greater purpose in the life that is behind it) has taken a giant step toward his own freedom and toward his recognition of his essential divinity.

At Findhorn, festivals are used as a means of integrating and uniting the community in a shared experience, emphasising our awareness of the great forces and cycles that move through life, and educating ourselves in the reality of the festival within and of the great story that seeks to be unfolded through the worlds of form.

What are the festivals that we celebrate? What is their meaning? At Findhorn, the festivals are geared, as were the ancient ones, to the aspects of Nature, because Findhorn itself is orientated to work in co-operation with the forces of Nature, the devas and the elemental kingdoms. Each of the festivals represents a stage in the cyclic manifestation of life and form, of life moving into form, learning of itself, moving out of form and then back again, the inbreath and the outbreath of creation.

The festivals begin with what could be called the festival of identification, the festival of identity. This is the winter festival and it coincides with the great human, divine festival of Christmas, the birth of the Christ. Let us examine this festival for a moment from both of these viewpoints. In the natural world, what occurs in the heart and depths of winter? To the outer vision everything is dead. Snow lies upon the ground — if one is where snow falls in the winter. Life has come to a stop, or so it would appear, and the earth seems to be in its period of greatest crystallisation. But if one could see behind this appearance, one would be aware that this is the time when life impregnates the earth and quickens the seed within the soil. It is the time when the earth, freed from the hurly-burly of the summer, meditates upon itself and affirms its true identity. Imagine yourself coming home from work. All day you have been involved with people and activities, and through this involvement you become a bit scattered. You come home and you take time to relax and gather yourself together. It is a time of meditation, a time of quiet, and yet it is a time of rediscovering and reaffirming who you are. So it is in the winter time of the earth. It is the festival of identity, of knowing that in reality there is only life. Beyond form, beyond time, beyond space, there is only life.

When we move from this natural view to a religious one, we see exactly the same drama being enacted in the birth of the Christ, for the Christ manifested as a man to show Man his true identity. In essence, the Christ message is: "Look upon Me, oh Man, I am yourself. I am your true self. I am the abundant life that is your true nature. Be what I am. Live my life." Before the Christ was born and came to work and stir amongst the sons of men, Man had identified himself very closely with form and matter. But through the Christ experience, the identification was made plain that Man is more than matter, more than a biological creature, more than just a transitory product of the actions of time and space. Man is the life of God, the Word made flesh, the Christ. Through the Christ taking birth within the vehicle of a highly e-volved member of the human family, the great Master Jesus, the Christ life entered to quicken the seeds of Christhood within the soil of all humanity.

The day shall come when all humanity shall move into the summertime, a full manifestation of the collective Christhood, but before this summertime comes there is the festival of Easter, the spring equinox, the festival of affirmation. In the heart of winter, life is received and the seed is quickened. It knows its identity as life and it knows its destiny, genetically and spiritually. Then begins the process of affirming this identification, and through this affirmation, spring is born, the bursting forth of the bud from the soil, the bursting forth of realisation and understanding from the soil of human consciousness.

We talk about a New Age. It might be said that the New Age is the festival of affirmation for humanity, the springtime of the Christ. Again this is a great Nature festival. Early Man saw it as the return of life to an earth that seemed to die in the winter. He used his festivals as a way of affirming and attempting to harness this life-giving energy, to overcome the deathlike states of the winter. Religiously we have this portrayed for us in the story of the Christ, crucified and then resurrected, and Easter is the great festival of resurrection.

In the New Age it will probably cease to be so, for resurrection is only a meaningful concept when death is a meaningful concept. On the other hand, the deeper meaning of resurrection is affirmation, the demonstration of eternal life, of that which has not died and which cannot die. This is what spring is all about, the affirmation of that which one identified with in the winter. It is in the festival of self-actualisation, of externalisation.

From this comes the great festival of manifestation, the festival of midsummer. This is the time when activity on a form level, on an outer level, reaches its peak. It is the time when Nature is most active on the outer. It is the time when that which was buried within the seeds and vivified in the winter and which is affirmed, actualised and externalised in the spring, can be seen and experienced. Therefore midsummer is the festival of experience. It is all about us. We can see the results of what we have planted. We can experience these results. Out of this experience come assimilation and wisdom. Were these the right seeds? How did the planting go? If they were right, then let us continue. If they were wrong, then let us learn and through this learning be transformed.

Thus there is the festival of transformation, the festival of assimilation, the festival of wisdom, Michaelmas, the autumnal equinox. This represents in Nature the time when the seeds fall; the product of the summer transforms itself to become the seed of the next cycle of identification and externalisation. It is the time when form begins to move toward quiescence, when death begins to move upon the land, death in the sense of transformation of form. It is the time when inbreath begins, the time of assimilation, of reflection; and as such it becomes the gateway again to the birth of the Christ in the festival of identification.

These four great festivals work out in Nature and in the life of the individual man. They are festivals of manifestation, of identification, of setting into motion the activities that grow out of this identification, of experiencing the results of what we have manifested, and of gaining wisdom and knowledge from that experience, the harvest which paves the way for future expression. Therefore these festivals have meaning on many levels—on natural levels, on psychological levels and on spiritual levels. They also bring into objectification the forces which they represent.

The Indians of the Plains of America had a tradition whereby an individual would receive a vision of his life. This vision would indicate the direction his life would take and the forces to which he could attune and draw into himself in order to make possible the fulfilment of his life destiny. But before he could truly tap these forces he had to objectify this vision in a ritual dance. He had to experience it in a symbolic story through ritual before the abstract potencies would be available to him.

In the same way, I may know a certain concept intellectually, but the power inherent in that concept is not mine until I understand it and have integrated it within my being, until I have experienced it. The festivals assist in this kind of experience.

The power of the Christ is well proclaimed through our religious traditions, but what does it mean to *be* a Christ? Most people will never ask themselves this question because they have been taught that the Christ is a being separate from themselves. However, the ancient wisdoms teach us that the Christ is a universal principle, the heritage of all humanity, and that the seeds of Christhood are within each waiting to be released. The question of what it means to *be* a Christ is a very pertinent one therefore, one which each person must answer if he is to draw the power of this Christhood to him and release it within his world. Thus the people who participate in Passion Plays, who take the part of Christ in drama, in theatre and films, often experience, if only for a short time, the impact of that life, and it is a transforming experience.

One of the most popular books ever written, one of the world's best-sellers, was a novel called *"In His Steps"* in which a group of individuals decided to live their lives as if they were the Christ. They asked themselves before every action, "What would I do if I were the Christ?" This transformed their lives and their society.

The Festival of Identity, the Festival of Christmas, ideally should give to each person the chance to experience the drama of the Christ identity, to live the story, to objectify the vision, so that the power of the Christ becomes real and meaningful in his life and he sees it as part of himself and not simply as an aspect of an historical story. Only a Christ can truly celebrate Christmas. Only one who understands that to celebrate Christmas he must himself participate in the Christ experience, knows what this experience is about.

Children play at being adults. They play house. They play at being doctors and nurses. They play various roles which they see adults in their world taking on and fulfilling. By so doing they learn of themselves and may begin to learn what these roles represent. They do not say, "I am only a child, therefore I cannot be a doctor, I cannot be a fireman, I cannot be an astronaut." They say, "Through the power of my imagination I can be whatever I wish to be. I can experience its essence even though the form may be only the form that a child can understand."

Adults have forgotten this. They see the great forces of Nature and of the universe as separate from themselves. Adults say, "I am only human. I am not a god. I am not a Christ. I am not the wind nor the rain. I am not the forces that cause the earth to tremble, the forces that move the stars in their orbits." People under the influence of LSD, however, and people who have experienced mystical states of consciousness, have found themselves at one with these very forces, have experienced that there is no difference between themselves and the forces that move within the earth and within the stars, the forces of the Christ, the forces of God.

Festivals are exercises in creative imagination in which men can take on the archetypal roles which best represent their true and essential cosmic nature. Festivals can stimulate this right use of imagination, the power to create the images that place one in contact with the greater realities of one's life. It is through the loss of this creative imagination, and the wonderment and attunement that it gives, that modern man places himself in such states of powerlessness and confusion. Thus the great festivals of the world, the great festivals of the cycles of Nature and human experience, stand in contradistinction to this loss of imagination and ask man to come forward as if he were a child again and to imagine and play and go deeply within himself to understand what is the vision that lives within.

Within each man is this inner festival, his own unique cycles and rhythms, his own unique place in the dance of creation. It is his dream, his story which he has come into life to externalise, to act out, to give form to. But men forget their story. They lose it. They lose their dream and their vision. They lose contact with *the festival within.* To participate in a drama or a festival it is not sufficient to remain only a spectator, only a body moving through some kind of activity. To allow the festivals of your society, religion and culture to communicate to you the reality and the nature of your own inner story and festival, is placing you in touch with the great sources of power, of life, of wisdom and of love that lie within you. The festivals can do this for Man on a collective level and can help each individual to learn to see life itself as a festival-like experience, thus enabling him more easily and clearly to draw forth the power and the nature of his inner dream.

In the New Age, Man will come increasingly into contact with his inner festival, the life of his creative spirit. Through this he will gain the power to transform his world, until every day, every moment is an expression of this great ritual and festival of joy, the creative dance, the song of God, the drama of creation.

Use the festivals that you experience in order to gain this understanding. Seek within yourself to understand the archetypal drama which you are here to fulfil and give birth to. The Christ life, which is your true life, calls you to the festival of itself and says, "The Springtime of Man is here. Let us identify with what we truly are. Let us affirm and through affirmation externalise this identity. Let us manifest the I Am That I Am, the being that we are. Let us be our festival and from it create new worlds, new dreams and new dramas."

"One way of looking at life
is to say that
everything we experience
is a symbol
behind which lies a greater reality,
a reality that cannot
be expressed verbally,
intellectually or physically,
but which is there nonetheless."

Chapter 2

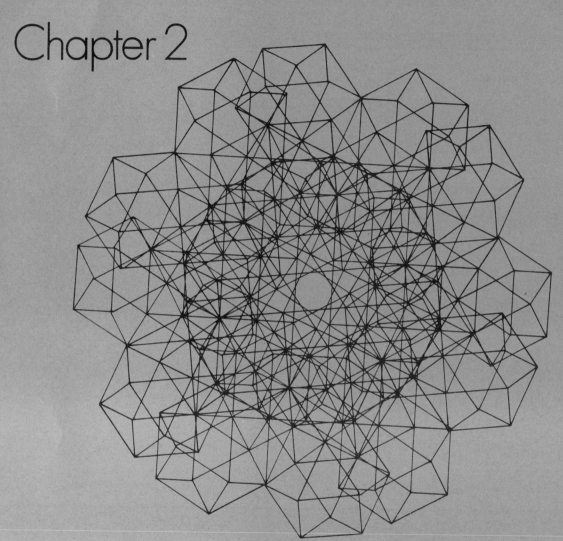

Winter: The Festival
of Identity (Christmas)

Christmas is the festival of identity. More than any other spiritual festival that man celebrates, Christmas holds the greatest potential power. The reason for this is that up to the time of the birth of Christ, the awareness of the Christ existed amongst mankind. As St. Augustine said, what we call the Christian religion has always existed, though it did not have that name until Christ was born. Probably 80 per cent of Christianity is derived from a stream of teaching, Platonic in its origin — before Plato, it comes from Pythagoras and before him it comes from the great unknown initiate whom collectively we know as Orpheus, and the Orphic traditions of ancient Greece.

In Western culture — and Christmas is fundamentally a Western festival even though in its present form, in its impact it is universal — our spiritual heritage was largely launched by the Orphic tradition because it was Orpheus — whoever he may have been or however many individuals may have borne that name — who began the process of investigating the mysteries of the soul, and presenting them to the people through the mystery dramas — plays, dance, music and so forth.

But, more than that, Orpheus took what had been until that time a very concrete approach to the spirit — that is, thinking of gods and goddesses in very literal terms — and he began to teach that all of these are symbolic processes relating to inner states of being. Thus he stimulated in the ancient Greeks the faculty of abstract thought, and out of that stimulation came a great percentage of our western culture. Pythagoras, Plato and Socrates were all Orphic in their spiritual orientation. These initiates fully realised the existence of the Christ, or what we now call the Christ, the Light within, and celebrated the birth of this Light upon Earth, within humanity, every winter; choosing the wintertime because it is the time when physical life is least active and spiritual life is most active. These initiates, through various means at their disposal, such as study, ritual, initiation and so forth, were able to lift their consciousness into attunement with what we call the Christ or at least awareness of it.

This awareness was very much for the few. Those who sought to enter the great state mysteries had to pass stringent initiatory examinations, so stringent in fact that if you failed one you were dead (which I suppose is an initiation of a sort). They had to ensure that the individuals to whom they entrusted the knowledge of the inner workings of nature—particularly because at that time man was much more attuned to some of the etheric processes within nature than he is now—were people of very high quality and standards, having great purity, great dedication, great strength of character and soul and will.

Those who passed these initiations entered the ancient temples which were not so much religious bodies as we would understand the term, but were a combination of university and church and government institution. These people were naturally regarded as a race apart because in many ways they were. They were semi-divine by virtue of having had awakened within themselves higher centres of spiritual power and many of the great initiates were regarded as God, or the children of God.

But the average man had no such self-image. He could see himself as being blessed by being human and having the opportunity of one day moving to a greater state, but he did not see himself as being the Light incarnate, the Word made flesh. Thus humanity (that is, Western humanity, and this is just as true for Eastern cultures as well) was really divided into two camps, into those who were the initiates, the heroes, the semi-divine individuals and those who were the ordinary race of men. The Light which we call the Christ was taught, was presented. Man knew of its existence and worshipped it in various forms but he did not identify with it. He had not reached the point where he could look upon himself in a general way and say, "I am the Christ."

When Jesus was born, this changed. The story which we have of Jesus is most likely not historically correct. It is simply a story of power, an initiate story, designed by illumined minds to convey certain meanings. Certainly Jesus was born a great being, a being who through many lives had prepared for the mission that was His.

There is no question about that. But he was not born the Christ in any greater or lesser degree than any other individual is. The chances are that, like any individual, given the opportunity, He could have muffed it. There was no guarantee that when the time came He would make that leap of being, that subtle change of consciousness, and by virtue of that know that He was the Christ. In esoteric teaching the Christ did not actually incarnate until the period of the baptism when the dove descended. But something must have led up to that; Jesus Himself must have gone through the process of bringing to birth the Christ within Himself.

When He did, when He was able through the best of His vision, the clarity of His insight, to say, "Why, I am this Light," then the Christ was born. I am not concerned in this chapter with other ramifications of His life though it is true that through His incarnation a great many other things took place within the realm of Earth, for He linked man and Earth and all the kingdoms of nature back to the single Life from which all life is sprung. Therefore there was actually impregnated into the etheric body of the earth an energy which had not been there before. The life of the solar logos entered into and infused more powerfully the life of Earth and the link Jesus made, made this possible.

What is important to us is how Jesus made this possible. Undoubtedly He went through various forms of training. Those of you who are familiar with the Aquarian Gospel know it goes into considerable detail describing the training He did go through. Various occult and esoteric societies throughout the centuries have spoken of what Jesus had to go through in the way of training: the various temples He had to go to, etc. etc. Undoubtedly some of that is true; some of it is propaganda, to make temple training seem a bit more glamorous, the same way that manufacturers get famous golf stars to endorse their products. But in point of fact when Jesus did what He did, He abolished the temple system and created a new form of spiritual achievement; and He did so gradually: He did not create it overnight. The great doors to the mystery schools did not close when He said,"I am the Christ." In fact they didn't close for three or four hundred years until the Emperor Justinian said,"You will close your doors," a purely political move on his part.

What happened was that Jesus fulfilled the law of His time and in so doing He set into motion a new law. He went through a long and arduous process most likely to bring the Christ to birth within Himself, but He went one step further and brought to birth the vision of a sacred life and of an identity which for the first time was able to bridge the gap between the initiate race and the race of men. Jesus said most plainly, "What I can do, you will do also, and greater things." All His teaching is exquisitely simple and remains to this day, if understood and applied, a very sure route to illumination. Divorced from history, divorced from the glamour of the supernatural, divorced from all the theological dogma that has encased it, the basic truths that Jesus presented—the power of giving, the power of love, the power of selflessness, the kingdom within and so forth which can be contained in a very small slim volume, offer more practical instructions in identification with our Source and with our Self than most of the books of occultism and mysticism and psychology that have come since. Man is really only now coming to a point where he can begin to appreciate the fact that he is the Christ.

Now he probably would have come to this sooner because this was really one of the teachings of the ancient mystery schools: Plato taught this, although not exactly in those terms—that Man was the living Light. When the Christian church began, as a church, it of course faced stiff competition from the pagan mysteries, the established religions in other words. And, quite crudely, the only way Christianity had a chance to survive was to beat the competition, to offer a bit more. This it did, because the pagan mysteries, that is the truly noble ones, demanded almost without exception long periods of training. They were highly abstract and subtle in their teaching and demanded a fully developed reasoning power. They were truly not intended for the common man, although they proclaimed the dignity of the common man.

Christianity, however, had something for everybody. Jesus was so simple and so direct that the common man could understand Him, could deal with what He had to teach. So the Christian fathers borrowed what they needed to borrow from the pagan mysteries (which was most everything) because Christianity is really not a religion. It has no cosmology of its own. It has no philosophy of its own. Jesus did not teach a religion, He taught a way of life. He taught a very practical ethical system the same as Buddha did. Everything else we have that is of a religious nature or a philosophical nature or a cosmological nature has come from basically Platonic origins. But, having taken it from there, the Church obviously did not want to let people know. After all, it is built on uniqueness. So it made a point of both discouraging and eventually destroying the ancient mysteries. Nonetheless those mysteries had taught this Light within and, perhaps, if there had not been the early competition and struggle for survival, that teaching would have come to man with greater impact before this.

But we are now at a point where we can appreciate the reality of Christmas. What Christ demonstrated was salvation through identification; if you want to be saved, the only thing you have to be saved from is yourself, your false image of yourself, an image filled with fear, with doubt, with limitation, with jealousies and anguishes and hatreds and all the rest of it. You can be free from that by stopping your continuation as a receiving being. Stop being a sponge, seeking to draw everything from life, and being fearful that you will not get it. Rather be a sponge that has been squeezed, and squeezed hard, that gives and gives and gives. That is Love. That is the outpouring, the outbreath, the actual taking of oneself in one's hands and generating the Light. Do not wait for it to come: create it. Christ may come and stand by the door and knock as opportunity, but there is no reason why He has to. We can rip the door off its hinges and go hunt for Him. Knock on Him, and say, "*We* are the Christ as well." Jesus did not come really as an initiate in the ancient sense though He may have been trained in that way. He came as Man, a Son of Man to show what men are capable of and to say, "The Kingdom is within yourself. Look there and find it. Seek it out above all things, and when you find it all things will be added to you." He knew the abundant nature of the human soul and the fact that all we seek, so spongelike, in our environment, is indeed within us.

As we enter our festival time, then, let us keep this thought in mind: that what we are celebrating is the birth, not so much of a Christ, but of a Man who discovered His Christhood, and identified with it, identified with His Source. "I and the Father are One." We think this hard because we are still in the process of mental evolution which is fundamentally very analytical. It sees things in terms of pieces and degrees and steps and small increments of motion and development, whereas the Christ is very synthesising. He sees things in terms of wholeness, of what is now, not how many steps it takes to get there or what process or what technique we have to use, but what is actually there now.

Our concept of the Christ has become quite intermingled with circus-like concepts of supernatural performance: He walked on water, and raised the dead and so forth. There may have been times when we wished we could change water into wine too! But that is not even the icing on the cake. It is hardly anything at all in a divine sense. In fact, it is quite detrimental if we interpret the Christ miraculously, for our tendency is not to interpret ourselves miraculously and therefore we create that division. On the other hand, if we see ourselves as a living miracle, then we do not place any barrier between what we are and what Jesus was and we are more likely to make that leap of identification. The Christ is not a "Hollywood Spectacular." He may be very subtle, very quiet. He is the Prince of peace. He may come very peacefully, very gently, in small things, almost always in small things. We can raise the dead, the death-like state in which we keep ourselves. We can prove our Christhood daily, in our mastery of our own being and through that mastery the introduction into Earth of light and love. As Jesus was a bridge between this and greater realms that Earth might be uplifted, so we can be.

This is why at Findhorn, there is such insistence upon perfection in all things, doing all things well, maintaining beauty and order and so forth; because it is the Christ task to uplift all matter and restore it to its own pristine knowledge of its beauty. Man can do this more than any other creature on the earth, for man has the capability of drawing beauty out of nature. When something is made well, when something is cleaned well, when something is planted well, when something is designed well, the Christ lives in it. It has been done with love. We have actually been a link between the life within that thing, whether it is a chair or a dress or a stove or whatever it may be, and the greater life from which it came. And by being that link through our love and interest, through our care and concern for perfection, we have infused that matter with life that it knew not that it had before. To that degree we have awakened it from slumber, and to that degree we also are the Christ.

The chances for playing this game of "I am Christ" are innumerable. And it should be a fun game, an exciting game. Let us see how many ways we can show Jesus that we are right up there with Him. We are making the identification too. He was not unaware of man's competitiveness. That is why He said, "All these things you can do, and greater things too"—the carrot dangling in front of us. But we think of the greater things in terms of spectacular things, when really the greatest things are often the most apparently insignificant.

So, again, during this festival time we celebrate the birth amongst humanity of a new rhythm of identification. The bridge has been built by Jesus (the gap between the soul and the slumbering of soul has been closed), and the kingdom of heaven is available to all men.

Christmas is an eternal festival. The Light is always arising, always being born and we always have opportunities for identification with the Light. Therefore let us use this time to open our hearts and minds to a greater rhythm, a greater understanding of what we really are, and so let us spread that rhythm to all our days and nights, filling them with Light.

Chapter 3

Spring: The Festival of Resurrection (Easter)

Man has come to think of himself as somehow separate from Nature and the world that has given him birth. But his roots in the natural world, in all of its cycles, are very deep and very powerful, and indeed provide for him the steps by which his soul can reach the highest.

Ritual in all of its forms also expresses the breath and life of Man's being as it seeks to transcend the limitations of the physical level and come to the freedom and perhaps the dwelling place of its highest nature.

From the most ancient times, Man has blended these two great forces together, the great and intimate cycles of the natural world and his desire to formulate and communicate his relationship with that world through the rituals of his heart, mind and body. But Man's links with Nature and with his past have not always been of the highest, for Man has not always shared the light, knowledge and wisdom which, though often seemingly shadowed, nowadays are so very much a part of our world.

Ritual is like our instincts, it is so grounded in the cycles of Nature from which we spring that when we move to a time like Easter, no matter how we view the particular Christian celebration which it represents, we cannot help but be part of the motion of ritual and of consciousness which this festival invokes out of human consciousness, because it is the festival of spring as well. It is a time of the rebirth of life from the seaming death of winter, and since Man is life incarnate, this coming again of life is very important to him.

For people attracted to a centre like Findhorn, where we seek to explore and to define the patterns that will become ours in the ages ahead and seek to understand the patterns of the past so that we can be free of them in some cases, and more integrated in others, it is good to understand the forces that are at work during this cycle, this festival, because they are far more ancient than the Christian dispensation. Because of our many links with the past, both privately and collectively, the impact of this most ancient of festivals is very much with us; but at the same time the impact of new patterns, new energies, also seeks to become part of our consciousness and our world.

Let us project back in consciousness to early Man who was much more intimately a part of the natural world than we appear to be, much more aware of the forces which populate forest and glen, valley and mountain, river and lake, much more aware of his relationship with the many powerful though unseen citizens of this planet, and aware of them in a most awe-inspiring way—the mighty gods who ride the winds, the lords of thunder, angels of lightning, those particular forces that seem to pull from the earth the qualities of life during the winter. All of these, understood or not understood, seen or invisible, yet remain to Man most awesome, and early Man, very much living in a pattern of the drastic distinction between life and death, was keenly aware of those forces which seemingly had little relationship to his human estate and which could so easily spell for him death and destruction. Man, in his early days of learning to come to terms with and to master the life forces of the animal kingdom and of planetary existence, was very much aware of the pattern of death, not necessarily always in a fearsome fashion, for death was so very much part of his life that fear was dulled by its very familiarity. Certainly its awesomeness was there. The death of an individual was something that could be recognised and understood, the death of a tree, the death of a flower—all these were minor events. But the death of the countryside, the seeming death of the whole planet, as winter and darkness descended upon Earth, this was something to be whispered about, to be taken deep into one's consciousness beside the campfire, to ponder its mystery and what it portended for Man. Who was to say, as the great veils of winter descended upon the countryside, that life would come back again? Perhaps the cycle had completed itself and whatever gods were involved had packed up their tents and stolen away into the cosmic reaches of life. Early Man felt himself to be very much at the mercy of these powerful forces in ways that are difficult for us to understand now because of the development of our being, and yet we still share the roots of that experience.

The passage of winter and the coming of new life, as the ground suddenly began to spring forth and to overthrow its apparent deathliness, was truly a miracle. This was an event calling forth more than joy, awe of the continuous defeat of darkness and death, and the alleviation of fear, as Man became aware that the time of darkness had passed and the light was returning. Once again Man could enter into the cycle of growth, of nourishment, of harvesting upon which his very life depended, for again, with the coming of the winter, his source of supply dwindled, and unless provision had been made, he too faced the death of his being.

Fear is a very ancient emotion in Man. Fear is intimately connected with the rituals of winter and spring, taking many forms: fear of darkness, fear of death. In the coming of spring, new life, new birth gave Man a sense of conquest over that fear, an ability to shrug it off, as we shrug off in the morning the terrors of the night before, although we know that the night-time will come again. So Man began to make his preparations in consciousness to deal with this cycle, to deal with death, destruction, darkness and the cessation of life. I am sure that in Man's early consciousness it seemed as though the earth was being drained of its very vitality. If only in some fashion this vitality could be returned to the earth, if only in some way the earth could be replenished with the life force, perhaps it might not bring the cessation of winter, but it might be just enough nourishment to get the planet through to the next spring. And Man began to conceive of the sacrifice of life, the giving of life and the descent of life into darkness and into death that there life

41

might grapple with the forces of death and darkness and prove itself, as always it must prove itself, the stronger and the greater. Who more right and capable of giving their lives than the strongest and mightiest, the godly, the kings, those who seem to have the most life force of the community, those who seem to have the most intimate connection with the gods, perhaps, indeed, were gods themselves in mortal form? Out of this developed Man's ritual of spring, which became the ritual of the sacrificial god, the priest king, the divine Being who gives his life that life might be perpetuated, who gives his body that Man might have nourishment, and who gives his blood that the earth might drink and not know the finality of death. Out of all the legends of Man's culture comes this pattern of his attempt to perpetuate the life force throughout the winter, or through whatever pattern of darkness represented for him the equivalent of winter in his own experience, by sacrificing that which was most vital, most unfolding, most divine.

In Egypt, for example, there is the legend of the death of Osiris and the scattering of his parts to the four corners of the earth. The Greeks, however, had a somewhat happier myth, of the abduction of Persephone to the caverns of Hades. She was forced to spend a few months with her new husband, the lord of the underworld, but was allowed to come forth again in the spring, and in her coming forth, all life rejoiced at her return, for she was the giver of life. Here again was the concept of life in its most pure and vital state, for surely there is no image more symbolic of the vitality of life than the virgin queen, the young girl who is in the prime of her fertility, with the ability to bring forth new life from her own being, but who is forced to enter the caverns of death.

In myth, in ritual, in consciousness and in experience Man sought to test and to demonstrate again and again the invincibility of life over all that would deny life, and the motivation behind so much of this is the pattern of fear and the awareness of death which, in itself, is the denial of life. As this pattern built up in Man's consciousness, a very strong and powerful thought-form developed which stated, "He who would be the greatest among you must face death and destruction, must enter the darkness and the tombs," for that is what Man has decreed out of his fear, that he must continually have a champion to protect him from that which is the essence of his fear.

When Jesus came, He brought what is truly the essence of a New Age message, the concept and demonstration of love. He merged into a society and a culture which was very much attuned to this particular pattern of the sacrifice of the priestly king, the high initiate, that from the sacrifice Man might be spared and life continue. I am sure that at a very early point in Jesus's ministry, He realised that, at that point of time in human culture, if He accepted the role of love, men would seek to make of Him a saviour, would seek to make of Him one to carry their burdens, a champion and light-bearer. If He accepted this role, then its inevitable consequence would follow. The saviours of Man are the sacrifices of Man, for it is in this way that Man has interpreted the necessities of salvation. Of course, Jesus accepted that role. He accepted Himself for what He was: a being of love, a human being, an individual who accepted His full birth-right and then allowed that to carry Him where it would, in fulfilment of Himself, and in service to those who were His beloveds. Whether it is historically correct or not, the ancient pattern fulfilled itself.

On Good Friday, we traditionally celebrate the sacrifice of the priestly king. We traditionally experience the destruction of that being whom we know must be destroyed if we are to live. It is a ritual which, in its deepest essence, is born of fear and is born of an awareness of death and darkness which, in some way, must be contested by Life and Light. Jesus could accept His pattern and role because, in His being, He was Life, and He knew that that thought-form, that pattern, had no power over Him. It had no more influence upon Him than a script might have upon an actor, no real power to penetrate His true being, but only the power to compel Him, either historically or allegorically, to take a certain role in the symbolism of human consciousness. It was inevitable, because of what He was, that death be conquered and life emerge triumphant, and all those who believed in that pattern could again partake in the sense of security, the release from fear, and the culmination of the ancient ritual: "The king is dead. The Saviour reigns. The Christ is crucified. Now Man may live."

Easter itself, the concept of the resurrection by which life proves itself triumphant over death, light triumphant over darkness, has a central meaning to the Christian religion. It is a core concept which states that whosoever believes in the Christ shall live and have eternal life, for death has been triumphed over, death has been conquered. Yet the ritual had its meaning not because Jesus was Life, but because He conquered death, and over the ages we have lost again the deeper insight into what transpired through Him and through others. We see it as being the triumph over death which is, of course, the acknowledgement of death as a fearsome presence, which must in some way be conquered by the champion of our choosing.

Jesus wore the colours of Man's soul as He went out into the jousting arena. It is a little bit like a rather gripping scene from the film "Camelot" in which Lancelot, going out to joust, takes up the Queen's colours. He is scorned by the Queen and by others because of his boastfulness and the fact that he is French and not really accustomed to English ways. He has said that he is the best. He is the Champion. He is the light. And on the field of battle he proves it. But in the moment of battle, he kills his opponent and, as he realises that his opponent has been killed, he picks him up in his arms and says, "I will you to live. You *will* live." His opponent opens his eyes and has been brought back to life. At that moment, the court is stunned and realises the purity of this being. Of course he gets the girl in the end too, so it all works out.

In a way this is what Jesus has manifested. Scorned and rejected as a man because what He taught and demonstrated was different from what had been anticipated, His conquering of death put Him in a favourable light. It gave Him good publicity, a good press, and ensured the historical position of the Christian church, giving it power. But the question which I put to you is: Do we celebrate the power of life or the power of death?

Occultly it is said that Easter will be the great cornerstone of the religion of the New Age because it represents resurrection, the movement of Man's spirit out of the tomb of matter, darkness, ignorance and superstition into the light of knowledge, divinity, love and awareness. However, I would suggest to you that *Easter will cease to exist as a concept in the New Age simply because death will cease to exist as a fearsome concept.* One does not send a champion to wage war against one's beloved, and death is only the veil over the face of the Beloved—and even that veil is being swiftly torn away.

I suggest a change of concept, that the creative season of the year is not spring, but winter. Winter is the most vital and productive season, for it is the time when all of life gathers itself into its creative centre and there releases the energies which will take form.

46

It is like saying, "When does birth take place?" Perhaps birth takes place when a man and a woman look into each other's eyes and realise that out of their love new life shall spring. In their awareness that they wish to move into oneness or to manifest the oneness which they already have, energies are released which shall unfold themselves in due course. Everything that follows conception is simply development. The baby that is born is only the more fully developed manifestation of that which was created at the point of conception.

So it is with spring. That which comes forth in this season is not the renewal of life or the reappearance of new forms after a time of death and darkness. It is simply the externalisation of that which was already created, made perfect and manifest on the inner during the incredibly creative silences of the winter months when all that is life does not cease to be life, but returns to its true living centre where it is one with itself, where it can be free from the distractions of dealing with form and matter and returns to its essence and, in that essence, knows what it is, unites with its own being, and from that uniting conceives the forms that shall beautify Earth and give nourishment to the forms of Earth in the seasons ahead.

In spring we celebrate manifestation, the manifestation of that which is already created. In spring we celebrate the reappearance of life, but only because we have not had the vision to see the continuation of life and the cycles of creativity. In the New Age

47

we gain that vision. That is what the New Age is all about. We realise that life itself is not cyclic. Its forms are cyclic, but life is continuous, always deepening and intensifying in upon itself in greater and greater creativity and exaltation. We realise that each day celebrates the emergence of life and the withdrawal of life, but that each emergence and each withdrawal is simply another manifestation of that same and continuous force and power which has no ending, has no cessation, knows no death.

Truly, for those of the Christian heritage, Easter will be used to launch the consciousness into the realisation of the invincibility and the continuity of life. However, a further step must be made beyond the resurrection, beyond the death, into the realisation that life simply does not cease; it only moves from its heart out to to its extremities and back again in eternal circulation.

Another task is laid upon us as well, for the thought-patterns of crucifixion and resurrection are strong, as is Man's fear which makes him require the champion or the sacrifice that he may be free. Those who come forth, whether individually or collectively, and courageously and knowingly take upon themselves the reality and realisation of what they are as divine Beings, accepting their messiahship and Christhood, come forth as saviours of Man; or rather, they come forth as demonstrators of what Man is capable of and, therefore, they are way-showers. All of these, either individually or collectively, will be faced with the threat of the cross and the spear, the ritual death in some fashion or other, not necessarily physically, for we have mostly gone beyond that, but in consciousness.

A great being who came forth in the early part of this century and was put forward as the new saviour of Man, whether he consciously realised this or not, intuitively knew that for him to accept that role would have meant his destruction as a being. So he did not accept it. That, of course, is Krishnamurti. What he did do was to shatter some of the power of that thought-form, although he did not actually create an alternative. He helped to sever the links that were preventing the new from manifesting, though he has not in all ways manifested the new, because of the timings involved.

In this community, people like myself, any individual who comes forward and accepts a certain responsibility relative to the evolution of Man's consciousness and soul, finds from all corners the forces that seek to claim his life and make of it a saviour for those lives who do not know the divinity within themselves. In a beautiful message received through Elixir, God said, "You cannot lean on any other. Each man's salvation lies in his own heart. The divinity of each man is in his own life, and the inevitability of life is in his own being and in his own keeping."

We must all seek to break the archetypal power of Easter, so that the true pattern of life which Jesus demonstrated may emerge. His whole life was His message, not His death and resurrection, which was, in a cosmic sense, simply a stage show to fulfil human expectation. We have the power, through the affirmation of life in all of its forms—human, vegetable, animal, etheric—to show that the time of the saviour being, the priest king or the priest group which can sacrifice its life to the whole, is past. The whole has never demanded sacrifice. It has only asked realization of what it is, for when we know what the whole is, then we are part of it, and we give to it joyously and continuously in the circulation of life which is the inevitable pattern of our being.

It is a new celebration which we seek, the affirmation of the continuation of life which, in the springtime and in the coming forth of bud and blossom, simply proves what has always been there, making it more evident to us, and inviting us lovingly, earnestly and powerfully to lift our vision of ourselves and of the Whole, to go beyond the bud and blossom, and to see the presence of the Beloved, Who is eternally there and within ourselves.

Chapter 4

Midsummer: The Festival of Manifestation

Not long after I first arrived at Findhorn, I had the pleasure, and in many ways the privilege, of being escorted by Divina out over the moors to the north west, to a place that is sacred to the nature forces. It is a hollow in the dunes surrounded by gorse, and we went there with ROC and two others. We had a meditation there. At the time ROC commented on the presence of Pan, on his overlighting being, and on his pleasure that human beings would take the time and the respect and the love to open themselves to his presence.

It was a very special half hour and I shall always remember it, though physically we did very little.

During the midsummer festival we all have an opportunity to share a very similar experience; for what we are celebrating when we celebrate midsummer day, midsummer eve, and this great natural festival of energy, is truly the celebration of Pan. It is that time of year when this great being is closest or most evident in his release of life through the earth, speaking now for the northern hemisphere.

Pan is the great shepherd god of ancient mythology, the god of the woodlands, the god of the elementals, the god of the life that courses through nature, the god of the sap that rises, of the seeds that burst forth into life, of the branches that bear fruit. He is the god of life, the god of abundance. He is cosmic in his scope but intimately rooted into the earth, and man, seeking to portray this, first saw Pan or conceived of him in a form that could match his immensity and yet his immanency: half animal, half man, half goat, half man—so Pan was conceived: a god who danced and played his pipes. His melody is the melody of life.

Throughout this celebration, and perhaps throughout all the days of your lives, I would draw your attention to this great being and the presence of his melody.

In the darkness of winter, life abundantly enters the earth, silently, beyond human vision. At a time when all seems most death-like, most still, most dark, the Life, the Light, the Presence of the Beloved is most active. It is then that the consciousness of the earth bends itself like a mother unto all that has been planted in its womb, and turns its energies inward in deep and potent meditation, that all these seeds whatever form they may take may be blessed with the presence of this life and be quickened.

Throughout the spring the processes of quickening gather their momentum; the casings of the seeds break, the life emerges, the soil is torn asunder, and the vision nurtured in the dark yet born of Light enters into visibility; so that on the longest day of the year, when outwardly the light is the greatest, we may look about and we may see what has been wrought. We may see the abundance, the mystery, the miracle that has emerged from the apparent death of the earth.

This is Pan's handiwork, and like any creator he is part of his

creation. There is a pride, there is a joy, there is a quality imposs-
ible to describe, but one which I know you have experienced if
ever you have created anything, a certain painful tenderness that
embraces the thing that has emerged from you. All this fills this
Being as he embraces the earth and offers up what has sprung from
him again in the great cycle of seasons as his gift to the cosmic
whole, as his gift to the Beloved, that the will and plan of God may
be continued. For if Pan withdrew his energies, the seed would not
sprout, the bud would not give forth fruit, the flower would not
blossom, the death of winter would be the death of spring and
summer as well. The great rhythms of life, which are the cosmic
feet that carry us to indescribable destiny, would be halted and all
that we know would come to an end.

But it does not end! Pan gives of himself, and from that giving
the rhythm continues, and the fruit of his giving is all about us at
this time.

This, then, is the festival of Pan, the festival of Nature. It is
the time when the abundance of the creative spirit is shown forth.
It is the time when faith, long nurtured, reveals itself not only as
the evidence of things unseen, but as the substance of things which
are seen.

It is the festival of manifestation, the proof of the presence
of God. It is the revelation of the longest day, of the unending
light. Therefore it is the festival of Truth. For however the sun

moves through space, and however the earth moves about the sun, and whatever the length of light and dark within the cycles of the year, there is this one truth: Light is.

"Light is. Light IS." Like unending streams that course from the summits of mountain peaks, light flows on and knows no ending. The Light that is made evident in the abundance of the summer, the same as is evidenced in the embrace of winter's darkness, the Light that is within the seed, the Light that is within the plant and the flower and the fruit.

When we move on in the year, like the stream we shall rejoin the ocean. The cycle will move yet another step; the abundance, the Light, will have moved through the form; and having been revealed, consecrated, and offered up in this festival, will reach its consummation of acceptance when the doors of autumn open and the cycles of inbreath begin. And in the winter it will be like the rain and the snow that fall on the mountain peaks, pure crystalline Light, seed Light, which shall in the spring melt again to reveal its unending flow.

Pan lives in rhythm. He is the poet of earth. He plays his pipes; and if we would share in his festival, then we too must hearken to the poet that is within us and to the dancer that stirs within our limbs and to the lover that flames within our heart and mind. There are no words that can do justice to the grandeur of this festival, and we as man are invited, nay privileged, to come in spirit and in imagination, in rhythm and the poetry of our love to the sacred grove of summertime to share Pan's presence and the rejoicing of his kingdom.

Man too can learn to rise on the melody of this great natural force back to his homeland. And more than that, man can learn to perceive himself as that which is child of God, but the ward of Pan who has guided and guarded his growth through the millenia upon the earth until man could mount again unto the stars and be the summertime of the planet. For in a strange way, as we come to understand our destiny as human beings, we approach more deeply into the mystery of this great festival and the celebration of Pan becomes the festival of man as well.

Summer is the time when in the warmth of light, when beneath the nourishing energy of father-mother sun, form springs forth to show forth the perfection that it is developing. It is the time of the blossoming. It is the time when beauty reveals itself. But within the heart of man is that same longest day. Man is his destiny, is the summertime of earth. Man is that which shall mount from the seedling state in which he yet resides to be the firstborn, the flowering of this planet, and take the light of earth back into the cosmos from which it has come. In some great and unimaginable future when the autumn of earth is upon us, man's summerhood shall be more fully revealed. We see about us, reflected in our natural kingdoms, our own destiny: abundance, life, joy, rhythm, vitality. All of these things are also man.

Man has had this revealed to him. Two thousand years ago, give or take a few years, the "Light that is" revealed itself on a planetary scope, in flesh. Man who has chosen to see the wintertime of human experience, the form, the soil and not that which lies within it, had his attention drawn to One who was the incarnation of summer, and revealed to man that if he looks as Pan would look, then man changes and becomes a being who dances beside the river on its trip to the oceans, and in his dance reveals the Light that is without ending, the Love that knows no circumscription.

I should like to share with you a brief reading from one of my favourite authors which I feel is apropos. This is from a very delightful book called "Jesus The Son of Man", and it is written by the Lebanese poet Kahlil Gibran. This book is a collection of various impressions which various people, contemporaries of Jesus, had of Him and of His impact; and this is the impression of Sarkis, an old Greek shepherd, called by his contemporaries "the madman".

"In a dream I saw Jesus and my god Pan sitting together in the heart of the forest. They laughed at each other's speech with the brook that ran near them, and the laughter of Jesus was the merrier. And they conversed together. Pan spoke of the earth and her secrets, and of his hooved brothers and his horned sisters and of dreams. And he spoke of roots and their nestlings and of the sap that wakes and rises and sings to summer. And Jesus told of the young shoots in the forest and of flowers and fruits, and the seed that they will bear in a season not yet come. He spoke of birds in space and their singing in the upper world, and he told of white hearts in the desert wherein God shepherds them. And Pan was pleased with the speech of the new god and his nostrils quivered.

"And in the same dream I beheld Pan and Jesus grow quiet and still in the stillness of the green shadows. And then Pan took his reeds and played to Jesus. The trees were shaken and the ferns trembled and there was a fear upon me. And Jesus said, 'Good brother, you have the glade and the rocky height in your reeds'. Then Pan gave the reeds to Jesus and said, 'You play now. It is your turn'. And Jesus said, 'These reeds are too many for my mouth. I have this flute'. And he took his flute and he played. And I heard the sound of rain in the leaves and the singing of streams among the hills and the falling of snow on the mountain top. The pulse of my heart that had once beaten with the wind was restored again to the wind, and all the waves of my yesterdays were upon my shore. And I was again Sarkis the shepherd, and the flute of Jesus became the pipes of countless shepherds calling to countless flocks. Then Pan said to Jesus, 'Your youth is more kin to the reed than my years, and long ere this in my stillness I have heard your song and the murmur of your name. Your name has a goodly sound. Well shall it rise with the sap to the branches, and well shall it run with the hooves among the hills; and it is not strange to me, though my father called me not by that name. It was your flute that brought it back to my memory. And now let us play our reeds together'.

"And they played together, and their music smote heaven and earth and a terror struck all living things. I heard the bellow of beasts and the hunger of the forest; and I heard the cry of lonely men and the plaint of those who long for what they know not. I heard the sighing of the maiden for her lover and the panting of the luckless hunter for his prey. And then there came peace into their music, and the heavens and the earth sang together. All this I saw in my dream, and all this I heard."

We who call ourselves the sons and daughters of God, and we who attune our hearts to the rhythm of Christ's heart, can find again in the meaning of this festival and this celebration our attunement to Pan's pipes, and to the melody of that life that courses through the veins of earth, that sighs within the clouds, and that echoes with thundering stillness in the heart of great peaks. For if we are the sons and daughters of Christ, the embodiments of his Light, the seed-bearers of his future, then we are also the children of Pan, and we learn to carve from the reeds that grow beside the streams of our own experience the pipes on which we shall play the melodies of our future, that all that has been planted within us may grow and emerge in the summertime of our fulfilment.

To ask for less, to play less, is to deny what we are and to cast ourselves into a wintertime never born from nature.

Let us then rejoice in this festival.

For aeons Pan and all his kingdom have lifted themselves and their gifts of form, the pathways through which life returns to life unto the cosmic whole. And in ancient times man rejoiced with this festival and rejoiced in the longest day of the year. But now we who lay claim to a New Age vision can demonstrate the reality of that vision by being ourselves the incarnation of that longest day.

In Christ the human fulfilment of Pan's cycles was made manifest, for Pan himself is an expression of the Christ. Pan is rooted to this earth, though he is cosmic, though the sun itself is his homeland, and though he nourishes himself upon the fruits plucked from stars beyond our vision. Yet he is rooted to this earth, and to this earth he shall remain until the last life within the last grain of sand has achieved its cosmic stardom.

But man is not so rooted! In man the message of the unending summer, of the youth of the eternal Light, of the Love that is abundance and of the Light that sings of joy, can go forth and play the pipes of promise in cosmic realms yet unrevealed.

So we come together to share, as once I had the privilege of sharing, the presence of Pan and the sacred outpouring of his creativity; and we can hear his voice saying to the Beloved, "This is what I have made for You and for Your glory and for the fulfilment of what You are within all the lives that You have given into my trust." And we can join with this, indeed *must* join with it, if we are to fulfil the New Age vision and can say to the Beloved, "I, too, reveal what I have made from the springtime of my new consciousness, from the seed of my humanity which You planted in me aeons ago. I lay claim now to the crown of my summers. From the crystalline hopes, the snowlike dreams that once fell upon etheric earth, and with the seeds of humanity I can reveal now, I will reveal now, the released and melted flow of the waters of Your life. Aquarius, the water giver. We are the waters poured out, the summer streams.

"This, Beloved, is what I make, that in our timing together I too will step forth and be the midsummer festival of Earth, a joy released unto creation. Then shall all that Pan has laboured to create find its fulfilment in what I am. Having earned the sacred pipes, I will go forth, a piper of the Beloved, to bring summer wherever I go."

MIDSUMMER BLESSING OF PAN.

Children of the One God, I bless you.
And I bless you in the voice of all my kingdom
Of all the lives that surround you, invisible yet present

Calling through the rhythm of their life
For your attention and your response.
You follow the Christ who is your shepherd
And is the fountain from which my kingdom draws its life.
But I am the meadow in which you graze.
Forget me not.
The wealth of earth is yours if you will but open to it.
These are my words.
Throughout the ages I am One with all that flows from
    the single source.
I bring wholeness.
As you follow your shepherds
Do not forget the meadows in which you graze
Nor those who give of their life and love that you may live
And have the forms in which your souls may find their
    nourishment.
Let us be whole together.
As my kingdoms extend their boundaries to God,
Join with us and know again the ancient brotherhood which
    you share.

You are elder brothers to my children.

Do not forget that they too dwell within your home,

And look to you for the demonstration of their future.

It is with great joy that we accept your love and awareness
poured to us.

May this time that you have set aside to celebrate this
summer time

Be a seal and a sign of the ancient covenant that is between
your kingdoms and mine

And let it signify within your hearts, our joint future.

You follow the Christ.

I am the gateway unto Him.

As you love the least of my children

So you open the pathways to your own goal.

Accept our help as we give it and let us be One.

My blessings upon you each,

Upon this Centre,

And upon the voice which your lives provide

That the ancient covenants of life upon this earth may be
once again proclaimed.

"If we listen, surely we can hear the magical sounds that come from the life that surrounds us."

Chapter 5

Autumn: The Festival of Transformation (Michaelmas)

In Chapter Three I spoke about the new role of the Easter festival in the New Age. I suggested that Easter was actually a celebration of death rather than life and probably would not move into the New Age in its present form. The concept was affirmed that the most creative period of the year is winter, rather than spring or summer.

I want to elaborate upon this, because we stand in this celebration of Michaelmas in polarity to Easter. If Easter is the gateway to manifestation, to the coming into form of various things, Michaelmas is the gateway to creativity and to the ability to form on the inner plane what needs to be formed, and to unite that creatively and lovingly with whatever womb-like system exists which, in its fertility, can bring forth in the following spring the forms that are created now. For this reason Michaelmas will undoubtedly be the festival of the New Age.

Let us consider the nature of creativity. What actually happens when we create? What is happening up at the pottery and the weaving studio and the craft buildings? What is happening throughout the garden, especially now that the garden is going into its winter season? Is there a loss of life? Is there a phasing-out of energy? Is there a decrease of existence?

The least vital of all the planes of being is the physical simply because the physical is functioning in such a restricted sense. The "life" of this chair, if I may call it such, is not apparent to us in the physical realm, because it has to manifest through this very restricted atomic structure of fabric, of wood, of whatever else is involved in the construction of the chair. But if one could see this chair with the eyes of the soul, one would see it vibrantly alive, dynamically alive—a consciousness of God which, if withdrawn for one millisecond, would cause the chair to disappear, to cease to exist. There is work being done to keep that chair in existence; it is not simply a static, inanimate object. That is what I mean when I say the physical plane is the least vital of all the planes simply because the energy is held within certain well-defined boundaries and limitations.

But as we go into higher realms, what we can call the realms of light—they are the realms of light because its energy is released, its vitality is more apparent, its creativity is more obvious and the scope of that creativity is greater—as we move in consciousness into higher realms, whether it is simply an emotional realm or a mental realm or a spiritual one, we discover within ourselves greater energy, more potential to imagine, to feel, and to relate to our lives and to our world. We do not relate to the full extent of our sensory potential, but even if we were relating to its full extent we would still find that, if that was the only level on which we were functioning, we would lose a great deal of vitality. Much of what gives us the vitality of life, the zest of living, the joy or the anguish, the agony or the ecstasy of existence, is emotional and mental. Pure sensory impression becomes augmented and amplified by emotional response, by mental interpretation.

Those are the realms where creativity takes place; those are the realms in which it is all happening, and of course on the higher realms beyond that. By the withdrawal of energy apparently into higher levels—as when we go into meditation in which the summoning forth of the higher powers gives the outward appearance of quiescence but is really very dynamic—by moving to these inner states of being, we are not moving into a more peaceful level, or a more quiescent one, we are moving into a more dynamic one. And by withdrawing the energy into those levels, we find the potential for true creativity being given to us.

I shall give you an example: if you are an artist and you want to create something, or a gardener who wishes to create something, and you are pressured by people in your environment, by events happening around you, you are unable to create. Your attention is too drawn into the outer. Too much is happening to you and you feel "I've got to get away, I've got to get by myself, I've got to get into an environment that's conducive to this creativity." What you are saying is: "I want to move into a wintertime consciousness. I want to withdraw my beingness from outer expression for a period of time in order to pull it together, as the modern expression goes; in order to give my creative energies a chance to coalesce and to take form and from that form to move out into my world. I want to summon, in other words, my creative power, with which I will impregnate, creatively and lovingly, the realms of being and in that creative relationship allow new being, new form, to take shape, knowing that once it does, it cannot help but take shape on the outer." The physical plane must reflect what exists on the inner.

When spring comes and we rejoice in Easter and the apparent return of life, it is good to ask ourselves, "Where did all that life come from?" We see the shoots coming up from the ground, the buds bursting forth. They are not materializing out of nothing. It is simply the visible manifestation of a long process that has been occurring through the winter, the true creative process, the process of cell division, of nourishment, of drawing in the life force and anchoring it within the heart of earth, within form, and allowing it to build and to build and to build until finally it takes the shape that we can recognize and relate to physically.

If indeed winter was a time of death and none of those processes took place, then we could not have a time of life. There would be no spring, there would be no resurrection, there would be no Easter. The whole concept of the resurrection is, in some ways, a mistaken one, born of man's misconception, of purely physical vision that perceives true creativity as death when the life force moves to its more vital levels.

The Michaelmas Festival represents the creative impregnation of the physical universe with spiritual energy. It is that time when the essence of wisdom, of experience, of life that has been gained through the cycle of experience of spring and summer is gathered up to a point. The life forces know what they have been through in one cycle and they know what they need to create for the next cycle. The energies are focused in and they penetrate the realm of new creativity. And in the incredible ferment of dynamic life which this penetration of light creates, which this penetration of wisdom brings about and which this penetration of gathered experience sets into motion, whole new forms, new life, new universes can come into birth.

The consciousness that man is asked to achieve in the New Age is a consciousness of being able to tap his infinite creativity; in essence, to be able at all times to embody within himself Christmas, Easter, the Midsummer Festival and Michaelmas. The energies represented in nature by these four cardinal points are brought into the timeless state of man's own soul and made perfectly available to him, so that he is creator, he is manifestor, he is assimilator; he is that which can dissolve what has been created to make room for new creation.

To me, Michael has always represented the power of the Christ as it brings things into manifestation, that is the creative power of the Christ. He is equivalent to an executive board or managing director, the one who takes the vision and makes it real, gives it form, gives it power, gives it motivation, takes it out of the quiescence of the Divine Imagination and motivates it so that it goes through its cycle of experience and returns to that Divine Imagination richly clothed in wisdom and realized potential.

In the theosophical traditions, the Christ is the World Teacher; and the concept of the world teacher, the concept of Messiahship, comes very much into harmony with the significance of Michaelmas.

The World Teacher is one who can summon forth into his consciousness the power which we celebrate in the Michaelmas Festival; who sees himself not so much as an instructor of the world but as truly an educator, who through a creative union with the earth as the Beloved draws out the stored potential of new life and new creativity. Who is such a being? Where do we find such a world teacher? He is all about us. He is constantly active in nature. He is constantly active in all natural processes, including those which maintain our own life. And he is potentially active in our own consciousnesses.

For many of us there will come a time, if it has not already happened, when we say, "Yes, I am this force. I am going to place myself now into a creative relationship with myself and with my world and by reaching up and attuning to the energies of the inner, the highly creative energies, the wintertime energies, so to speak, I will release them through the springtime and the summer of my daily life, of my expression. By doing this, by opening channels for the release of the world soul, the world potential, just in that little bit that is before me, whether it is something I am making, whether it is a dinner I am preparing, whether it is an individual with whom I am relating, I can draw out of that situation a release of the world soul. I am, then, a world educator, and I accept and begin to wear the mantle of messiahship.

If we begin doing this, if we accept this energy unto ourselves, it will do strange things to us, because it demands of us a recognition of the splendour of what we are and of the cosmic potential that we incarnate. At that point we are confronted with a world that is seeking desperately for its educators, for its messiahs, but does not know how to seek them correctly. It wants them in a separative role, it wants them not to come too close, not to make any personal demands for change, for transformation. It says, "Lead me. I will stay the way I am, but lead me into the promised land. Lead me into the New Age. Teach me what I need to know." That is a rather mental approach to it all.

We confront, then, the challenge in our own being of being able to say, "Yes, I am this. Why deny it? God has never denied it. This is why I have come into being. This is the essence of my soul, the heritage of my spirit, the promise of my seasons of life. I cannot fulfil my human destiny until I accept this and give it birth and manifestation, until I become Michael in action, Christ in being.

Then we must be prepared, if we accept this, for what the

world does. The world does not particularly want to crucify people; the world wants to enshrine them, which is worse. But it is what many of us will encounter and we will need to find the balance of our own perspective, of who we are and where we are, and then we will need to find the balance of working with the world's consciousness to draw out of it the true vision and realization which are there, in spite of everything the world's consciousness tries to do for us or to us.

Each being is asked to be able to accept his at-oneness and identity with the world teacher, for, after all, to each of us we are the centre of our world. Can we not draw out of that of which we are the centre, the perfection which is inherent? If we begin doing that for the microcosm, we cannot help but do it for the greater macrocosm. Then people will no longer say, as it is written in the Bible, "Lo, there is the Christ." "No, lo, there is the Christ," and run here and there claiming to find the Christ here and there. Rather they will move to the consciousness that says, "Yes, he is everywhere, in me, in you, and in everything else."

We are not discussing metaphysical abstractions. We are discussing the very substance and essence of our life, of our identity. Each day when we seek to express ourselves, however we seek to express ourselves, we are performing a Michaelmas ritual. We are the power of manifestation striving to be released. This festival is the festival of our life. And it is particularly a New Age Festival because in the New Age we are not asked to reach up to the Christ, in ascension; we are not asked to move into another realm; we are asked to draw the whole thing down into manifestation, so that it becomes a living part, a living reality, a living vision on this realm, through our efforts, through our vision, through our lives.

So we stand here symbolically and in terms of the seasons of the year at a gateway to what is really the most creative time of the year, perhaps not creative on the physical level, but a time when all the inner processes go on that make apparent physical creation possible.

This brings up an interesting point that we are discussing things from the point of view of the northern hemisphere. In the southern hemisphere they are just moving into spring; so we again have the balance of polarities and the wholeness being made manifest. What is Michaelmas to us is Easter south of the equator. What is Easter to us is Michaelmas to them, in terms of the energy flows. So the wholeness is manifested upon the earth and on the same day the festivals are brought together and are the same thing.

Man holds this capacity through his own wholeness to draw the whole processional of the seasons, of time, of space, of experience, into that point of love within himself where it is all one and from that point relate to his world through love, through wholeness, through oneness, to take unto himself the reality that is always his, that of world educator.

Chapter 6

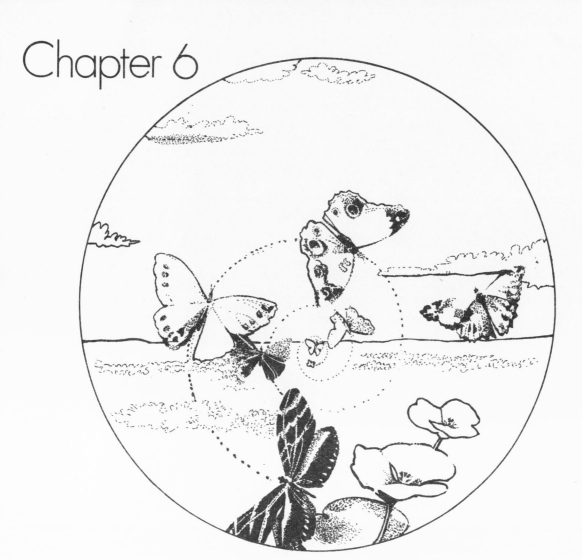

The Joy of Festival

Realise that you are expressions of spirit. You have taken up a temporary residence in a dimension of great restriction for spirit. It is important that you are not left untended by the qualities of your homeland. It is important that you are not left to fall completely prey to the downward spiral of matter and its directed energies.

There exists a quality which, for want of a better term, has been called bliss. It is a very lively energy. It moves just as light moves sparkling on water. It shrugs off all limitations and lifts the being back to its homeland. At the same time, this energy can accompany the being into the realm of matter. It is important that it should do so for it is this effervescence which prevents matter from destroying itself through too great a concentration in upon itself. The Masters, as you call them, are without exception joyous beings and are the very embodiment of bliss. They are laughter made flesh.

Man is a composite being. He is like a solar system drawn about a central sun, the planets being held in their orbits by the power of gravity. Man is a centre which holds to itself qualities of consciousness which before they were joined in him, had been incompatible. It is necessary for Man to have the power of concentration and of work in order to hold these patterns together.

But Man requires release. He draws energies into himself to accomplish his task and some of these patterns cannot be released through work, but only through his ability to attune to the effervescence of spirit. This may be done emotionally and mentally through a simple release and outpouring of joy, of fun, of laughter, but Man himself is asked to become the embodiment of this effervescence, the court jester of evolution. Man is asked to be the embodiment of many energies to fulfil his Godly task, and one of those energies is that of upliftment and the sparkling effervescence that moves through creation and indeed provides much of the momentum and motive power for evolution. In an ideal sense, everything that Man does is filled with this sparkle and effervescence and the barriers between work and fun dissolve. However, it is necessary for Man to have periods of time when he deliberately invokes the energies of effervescence, of laughter and of joy, becoming one with them, travelling forth on their rhythms and carrying their rhythms into his daily patterns.

Because Man's patterns have been held, to a great extent, in bondage to the requirements of form and matter, when he does release, he does so with that extremity of action which swings him out of balance. He loses control. It is not the steady rhythm of bliss moving through the life, but moments of great joy and laughter followed by moments of drudgery, greyness and despair. It is this swing from one to the other which must be counteracted. It is not giddiness that one seeks, but the rhythm of this creative effervescence and sparkle of life which permeates all to which the being turns his attention and energy.

You will find that the New Age is an age of working consciously with energy and providing outlets for energy release. All festivals, truly conceived and manifested, are necessary, because in their own fashion they are part of the great rituals of life. They are periods in which people come together in blending to create and release into the world the energies of upliftment and effervescence, of laughter, song and dance. These periods are the product of the work pattern that has preceded them and that follows them into an even rhythm. They are not necessarily a regular pattern, but they are absolutely necessary until the being reaches a point in which everything is bliss and pleasure.

You must learn that laughter is an energy in its own right and has its creative uses. The one who never laughs is not a completed being. You will find that the New Age will be an age of festivals, far more than what has existed in the recent past. It will blend itself into the steady rhythms of life in such a way that every moment is a celebration of the festival of living. Truly it is only Man who holds the concept of work. It has no correspondence in Nature amongst the devic and elemental worlds which live in a state of perpetual celebration, joy, laughter and festival. You have not yet appreciated the full power of joy and laughter, because you use it as release from the bondages in which you place your consciousness. You do not yet use it creatively as a form of work in itself.

It is an important aspect of the Laws of Manifestation, for God created and laughed as He did so and spun about in an infinite dance. Man creates out of the grimness of his spirit and the necessities that beset him, and his creations lack the ability to uplift him and attune him to his true heritage.

Eventually everything that is done should hold within itself the vibration of laughter and of effervescence. Eventually you will come to a point where anything that is not created in this fashion will be unworthy of you. Laughter moves in silence. Effervescence moves in stillness as well as in outer action. It is not emotional or mental release, but a strong and powerful rhythm of the sense of joy, participation in a continuing celebration of life and creativity. Living should be joyous. You will find that the festivals will initially serve to remind men of that. There are far more creative purposes for your festivals which are to invoke energies and make them available. Why not have festivals of manifestation, celebrating the gifts of God, celebrating the reality of that of which you have need, allowing your joy and laughter and your uplifted spirit to flow to the thought-forms you have built, increasing their capacity to make manifest? Laughter has the ability, truly expressed, to dissolve barriers. It is the great linking quality and is an expression of love. This is not the laughter that is the product of Man's critical side or his competitive side, but the true outflow of the joy of being.

You will find in the future that you will hold many celebrations, and you will be joined in them by Beings from other dimensions linking consciously with the overlords of Nature. There will be grest festivals in which Man and spirit and devic and cosmic Beings beyond unite and great creativity takes place. Your festivals should be worthy of as much attention of consciousness and creative manifestation as anything that you build. Those who become the festival makers, who are attuned to those energies and can make them real to others, are every bit as important as builders and craftsmen. Their beings and consciousnesses must learn to build the temples of joy and fun and laughter and to materialise them from the higher planes in order to bring these energies down where they can be sensed and utilised for healing, upliftment and transformation, for the cycles of your labour are uplifted by the cycles of your joy and the same thread is seen running through both.

To a great extent festivals will be linked with Nature but there will also be purely human festivals celebrating triumphs of human consciousness. Your Christmas Festival could be a most powerful experience save that you have turned it into a second-hand celebration. You celebrate an event of the past and an event which occurred to someone else. You do not celebrate the reality of the Christhood, nor its birth continually within you. If you were to do so, in great joyous concentration upon this, through song, dance, drama, music—whatever ways are meaningful to you at that moment to invoke and express these energies—you would find your consciousness being greatly aided in their externalisation of the indwelling Christ.

You will find festivals being used for healing. You will find festivals being used for initiatory celebrations designed to uplift people and to link them with the forces of realisation. You are surrounded by a continual festival. The festivals you create as human beings are your gateways into this world that surrounds you and your linking with this special form of power. It is an important thing to link with. You will find that your festivals will be greatly spontaneous, but there will be those who will work ahead of time, to form on the inner the channels for the energy to flow through. Nothing operates through chaos. All obey the Laws of Manifestation. When you rehearse, when you are preparing, you are obeying the Laws of Manifestation. This will become a conscious pattern in which the drama, the music, the nature of the festival is established on the etheric, thus opening the gateway. The energies that pour through will lift you into the realm of true creative spontaneity. Because you look upon these patterns as simple release, a break from drudgery, you do not yet realise their full power and you are using them to a minimal extent; but if you approach them with as much dedication and awareness as you approach any of your patterns, you will discover a source of power and illumination. They are worthy of your attention.

You should take your fun seriously and you should take your seriousness with uplifting humour. Laughter used properly is an energy of initiation. Festivals need not be funny, but they must move the consciousness into the rhythm of the uplifting streams, the fairy streams, the elfish streams. You have the legends of the fairies dancing about their circle and Pan playing his pipes. Understand the implications of this. True festivals are ritualistic, at least in the planes of consciousness. They invoke energy. They are like great dances, great wheels spinning, in which energy is drawn in and released. As I have stated, you are surrounded by festival, a special form of energy and power and creativity which Man has not yet fully learned to tap. It is very much part of the New Age and needs to be explored as the timing becomes right and you develop the means to do so.

There will be great festivals of the imagination, for Man's imagination is as yet an underdeveloped creative tool, but it is his link with divinity and his salvation. There will be festivals of fantasy, festivals in which you embody archetypes of creation and make them real. You have only begun to tap what is possible. Consider a festival in which people take parts, embodying, as it were, the different energies of creation such as the gods of Olympus. Man holds these archetypal symbols of power and of beauty and as he gives them flesh and fulfils certain of the archetypal patterns and legends, such as the legends which you have of King Arthur and the glory of Camelot, you are releasing into your world and into your lives the energy which these archetypes represent. When you celebrate Christmas, you are at least giving some entry to this energy. You will learn to do this to greater degrees in the future and you will find that you have tapped a limitless source of power for manifestation in all fields of the human endeavour.

Laughter is the spirit of levity, of levitation, rising up the spiral of life, whereas the power of gravity and of seriousness pull downward on the spiral. Laughter, properly used, lifts men, and all that you do with laughter, whether it is of the voice or of the spirit that flows through you, will contain this energy and will be able to radiate it out to all who contact it. The beauty of the plants which you see is due to the fact that they were made with laughter and with joy. They are the product of the natural festivals celebrating the goodness of God and His abundance.

The time will come when Findhorn will demonstrate the wholeness of joy. It will be known as a place of laughter where much is accomplished and all that is accomplished sparkles because it is done with laughter. Laughter is a rhythm of being. It is not always sound. It is not always gesture. It can be silent. It can be still. But it is powerful and has no limits to its capacity to uplift, heal and bless. Its purpose is to reveal one function—the joy of the New Age, not its pressure, not its gravity, but the upliftedness which is known throughout all of Nature and which Man now seeks to discover. All things move in balance. You are here to pioneer the attributes of the New Age and of the Seventh Ray, and festivities are very much a Seventh Ray expression.

Chapter 7

The Festival Within

We have been through many ages in the past, as a civilisation, as races, as cultures. We have achieved different states of mind, heart, and being. We have learned to master the rudiments of technology. We have learned to explore and chart our world. We have learned to elevate our concept of God and of our worship so that we cease to sacrifice ourselves or our children at various altars, but give of ourselves in love towards the great fellowship of life.

But all of this has been leading to one point where Man can stand forth from the environment of this planet, emancipated from all within his own consciousness that holds him in bondage to external forms ot any kind which prohibit him from perceiving and bringing out into the open, through his actions and his expressions, the limitless possibilities of divine life and creative splendour that lie within him.

We have come to a time when the focus is on Man himself in a way that it has never been before, but not Man struggling to become the conqueror of his world. This has been the focus for the past several thousand years, as Man has striven to survive and to prove, at least to himself, that he is the lord of Nature, the lord of this planet. It becomes increasingly evident to us that that course leads only to extinction for humanity.

Man is indeed a lord of life, but he is not the conqueror of life. He is not the conqueror of anything, not even of himself. Along that route lies ultimate disaster, whether it is in the disruption of the inner ecology or the outer one, the inner state of being or the planetary state of being. Instead, Man learns to focus on himself as a co-ordinator of life, a synthesizer of life, a point within which all the diverse streams of expression, light and dark, hot and cold, the various colours, the various emotions, the various thoughts, all the infinite diversity of living, can find its wholeness, its oneness and its release into perfection.

Man can no longer be the soldier, the conqueror leading his triumphal processions through the streets of being, but becomes instead the festival master, the one who establishes, in his own heart and mind, the awareness of the rhythms of life which are joy, peace, trust, love, wisdom and light. Freely and openly Man calls to himself all of life to partake in this festival within, in which everything is brought to its perfection, its beauty and its wholeness. Man has sought in the past to learn of his strengths, but only those particular strengths that would enable him to master his world. He has not sought to learn of those strengths which enable him to blend with his world.

As a humanity we now seek to learn how, in our personal lives and in our collective lives, we can once again establish our harmonious rhythms with our natural environment. But even that concept is a bit distorting, for it is also necessary for us to realise that we are infilled by Nature. We are not an artificial being; we are a natural being, an organic being. The rhythms of our own bodies, the flow of our circulation, the rhythm of our breathing, the blinking of our eyes, the movement of our muscles, are all a natural expression, every bit as whole and organic as the trees and the flowers, the wind that moves through them and the rain that nourishes them.

What is our own nature? And can we be at peace with it on all of its levels? Surely Man's intense drive to conquer Nature is at least a by-product of his intense drive to conquer himself, to subdue his own natural rhythms and to make them subservient to will, although Man throughout the ages has not fully understood will. I do not think any of us could look upon Nature and fail to see will in manifestation—true will; the will of knowledge, of knowing; the will of love; the will of timing; the will of such irresistable joyous unfoldment that when a seed begins to sprout there are very few forces that can halt its sprouting unless it is deprived of nourishment. The will of a seedling is a will that is not in opposition to anything; it is a will that is an affirmation of what it is. Seedlings are seeking to affirm what they are and the life within them, because there is no greater power on Earth than being the fullness and the wholeness of what God has given us to be.

Within Man, throughout the ages, there has been the promise of the festival of his own life, of the realisation of what he is and where he is. But he has consistently overlooked this festival in his rather military approach to accomplishment, achievement and mastery of his world. This has served him well up to this time. But the man who sets himself in opposition to anything is the man who is himself opposed; and his energy, from that point, becomes caught in the struggle and he loses sight of the festival of being.

Now the New Age comes. The whole motion of the Christ at this time is to awaken Man to the festival of his own life and the affirmation of his own being and strength. Out of that affirmation everything comes, whether it is art or music or dance or drama; whether it is his businesses, his sciences or his culture in general. It all flows from what he is. The ideas of a few as to what Man's culture should be, which are sought to be imposed artificially on Man by the mind, are not permanent. That which remains as the essential culture from which we spring is that which springs from the essence within us.

We are asked individually to be very aware of the festival within ourselves and what it means—what it means to be here at Findhorn; but even beyond that, what it means to be anywhere, at any time, because it is truly a universal concept we are dealing with, not a Findhorn one; except as Findhorn itself embodies a universal spirit. We use this community as a springboard into the wholeness of human consciousness and, as such, our reaching out to Man and the outflow of our being must partake of this universality. It does this, not through any attempt to please all people or to be at one with all people, but by our ability to anchor ourselves in the human essence of our being, what we are in our fullness.

When a seed is planted it fulfils itself. Man is a seed planted on this Earth, and he will fulfil himself no matter what layers of concrete of consciousness or of outer impositions are laid upon him. His springtime is upon him and no force will inhibit the fulfilment of his being. Out of that comes culture because that is the universal centre that we hold in common. Out of that comes the new civilisation, out of our ability to intensely and creatively aware of ourselves in the moment, not fearful of the future, not prescribing the future, not fearful of the past, not bound to the past, but alive in the moment to the festival of life that is going on all about us.

If we listen, surely we can hear the magical sounds that come from the life that surrounds us, the tinkling of little bells that bees wear as they go about their work, the whispering of fairies one to the other as they dart in amongst the leaves of the gooseberry bushes, the rustling of little gnomes and little elves as they scurry amongst us, and the deep, powerful, steady rhythms of our own heart and mind as we seek to affirm in each moment, often in spite of ourselves, the reality, the power and the splendour of our living and of our life.

The actual forms of festival are unimportant. The festival is continuous. It offers to us release from the past, release from the future, entry into the Now where we find the fullness of our human divine capabilities, our limitlessness.

A festival is a time of joy, a time of sharing, a time of song and mirth and dance, all of which is simply the outer manifestation of an inner state of being. These outer manifestations will not create that inner state of being. If we go through a festival waiting to be entertained, waiting to be made happy, waiting to be brought to a state of laughter and excitement, we shall probably be disappointed. If the festival of the inner life is to have any reality for us, then it has its reality because we learn that we are the festival and we release it into our life.

We are not the audience that sits back and waits for life to entertain us. This is a universal concept applicable to all men in all conditions. We either move through life as the festival master or we move through life as the audience, ceaselessly waiting to be entertained and often waiting in vain.

Throughout the ages, Man has created various mythologies, images of strange and magical places to which his heart longed to travel. Here at Findhorn we live in such a place. In the great opportunities we are given for fellowship, for communication, for creativity, for working with the Nature Spirits and with all the great elemental, devic and angelic forms of life, we are in such a place of real magic. The festival is a gift of awareness to us so that we can grow, not in our bondage to this centre but in our understanding and release of the magic of life itself of which this centre is such a great prototype.

This is a new age—because our focus turns to Man in a new orientation and we begin to look within and about ourselves to see what is the magic that is there, what is the splendour that is there, what is the joy that is there, what is the inner festival, and how we can, in our relationships with others, make that magic, that joy, that festival increasingly real until, as it has been promised, the whole world becomes the place of joy that it essentially is, and all men dwell in the eternal festival.